Find Your Color

Find Your Color

Lindsay Sfara

For more information, please contact via lightwingpublishing.com.

Published by Lightwing Publishing, LLC, an imprint of Lindsay Sfara.
1114 N Court St. 101, Medina, OH 44256
lightwingpublishing.com

ISBN 979-8-9941364-0-9 (pb) / 979-8-9941364-1-6 (eb)

Library of Congress Control Number: 2026928306

From helping climb over rocks, to throwing them in my way,
you were a part of this book coming to be.

So, regardless if friend or foe in my life, thank you—
and I forgive you (you know who you are).

My journey is because of you.
I'm here because of it.
And this is for you too.

Table of Contents

intro

The trees look safe.

She sees them through the glass. Her thoughts float to them from home, and from the car driving her to places she doesn't want to go to. They look safe, more than the walls and roof that guard her bed and family.

The trees look secure. A place she can play with joy. A place she can be herself. There's no caring about big, prideful homes to visit, and their reminder of what she lacks inside her own home. No caring about the posh dress and tights. But voicing against the homes, especially the dresses, scares her, even if she resents instruction on "acting properly."

She wants to be her.

But she must change to act—be—what they demand her to be. She must change who she is, be false shades of her to meet each view.

Her home is one for chameleons. At least, she has to be one to survive.

She has to change her color for each expectation. The trees stray too far to escape. Yet if they weren't, she'd not know what to do next. She may wish to hide from these burdens, but she doesn't want to be alone.

She wants to be loved. And that's why she stays.
But she must play the chameleon that hides who she is for that love.

Does it have to be this way?

Is the entire world, where the trees live, this way?

part i

Child, today you have to wear black.

It is proper. It is elegant. It is maturity. No one cares about your young age. You must act how they want to survive.

A proper lady does not bounce or kick her legs in the air while she's seated.

A proper lady wears the dresses and tights you so despise. Get over it.

A proper lady walks, never runs. Sits still, never plays.

But I don't want to go! It's so boring. They don't let me do anything. I don't like this dress. I don't like these tights!

Don't whine, child. A lady doesn't whine.

But I don't want to act like a lady!

Then they don't love you, and you don't survive. Are we understood?

. . . *Yes.*

Yes, what?

Yes, Ma'am.

break influence

The child crawls from ash.
Hope lost down her cheeks, frown tight.
Broken. But breathing.

—*Unfinished*

I gaze to the stars
glinting warmth at my soul's doors.
"Reach. Reach for us, child."

—*Worthy Stardust*

A new day declares the performers
to begin the act—start scene.
The curtain rises with the sun.

Stir awake, dress suitably for public,
commute, conduct work, commute,
collect valued paper—the ball and chain.

Voice-cracking youths drown under standards,
laboring for the promise of better decades
where mind and body age to weariness.

This is the mediocre playwright of society.

The script demands living days without flaw,
without doubt on one's "path to success."
Doubt creates loss and falling behind.

So cries the desperate plea of one
to succeed like other performers,
to know their own place on stage.

Yet how lonesome "fitting in" is,
ignoring their inner being for this play.
After all, the play is all that matters.

Until the illusion cast by Society is dispelled.

There is more to living than labor until death,
than the value of paper labeling worth,
than acting in the play's rendition of success.

Society's play does not heed the call
of a performer's true place on earth.
That is where you start your own play.

—*The Theatre of Society*

"You want a robot?"
New thoughts break my circuitry.
"I'm not a machine."

—*Static Shock*

You see my **lifespan**, my **profile**,
on that **plain** paper with ink.
Am I enough to you to reach the **alps**?
Or will I, to the **seafloors**, sink?

Hire me. Adore me. I will not **fail**
like other **finless flops**.
I'm no **spoof**, I'm **proof**
that I can help reach the top.

Now my progress shows my worth,
so why the constant **aloofness**?
You treat me like a **napless** babe
who's chastised for **loopiness**.

After all the good I've proven
in this **profession**, I feel small.
You're not a leader, you're a **felon**.
And now, it's **personal**.

I'm done with these **flips** and **flaps**
and **poofs** of worker-bee magic
just for praise from life **poisoners**
and **sponsorial** antics.

Why did I not do this sooner,
to cease priority of your opinion?
Take this **final** inked paper from me
and be gone with your **aspersion**.

—Corporate ***"Professional"***

Be not afraid, friend,
to stand onstage for yourself.
For no one else will.

—Lead On

This is my life, my tale, my stage.
Do you believe you direct it?
Your control is sourly unfit
to read my lines and turn the page.

Your influence is more a cage
that binds my light should I submit.
This is my life, my tale, my stage.
Do you believe you direct it?

Keep your place in my tale—backstage.
Your role is what I choose to knit
with woven words I deem befit.
I am my director, my sage.
This is my life, my tale, my stage.

—I Am My Own Play

You have no hold here.
You did not teach me power.
My power is me.

—The Credit is Mine

Imagine one step
bringing life's treasures yet reached.
You can make the walk.

—First Step

part ii

Today, my color is blue.

Their yells are like the door isn't shut, but my brother and I have it so. To hide us from what makes us scared. We always think the door can shield us. But it never does.

Blue is the color to hide alongside our things at home. To blend into the walls and under the bed. Maybe today the family won't find us. Maybe they will fight, stop, and the day will go on. Maybe we can keep playing—but quietly and to ourselves. If we are quiet and stay good, maybe their yells won't catch us.

We don't know why they yell at us. We can't tell what we do to start it. Some days we're together as a family. Happy. But most days, there's yelling and crying and blame. Happy becomes scared and we don't know why. Adults are angry at us, at each other, and we have to hide. We turn blue so we can't be found. We hope.

So if we stay away, if we aren't seen, then there's no hurt.

If we are alone, playing quiet and good, like they don't know we're here, then we're safe. We don't do or say things around them so we don't get scared. We stay blue. Alone. This is how we're happy.

But I don't want to be alone. I'm making them happy by being quiet and good. Right? And making all of them happy means I'm loved and not alone. Right?

Then why am I alone?

break fear

It feels heavy on your chest,
being engulfed in a thick shadow,
and having it seep into your skin.

It feels sickening
as it slows the body, mind, and spirit;
and everything is a dull numbness.

Shadows teem over the world.
All is gray and black
and not a thing seems right.

Days pass.
Months pass.
You watch it all go.

It's like watching a movie,
and yet, you're to be the lead role
and not a mindless bystander.

It's lonely.
It's empty.
It feels like something is wrong with you.

But something still flickers within
despite the thick darkness
and poison inside.

It's a new, playful idea,
the smallest of smiles on your face,
and a ray of sun from the sky.

Thoughts become lighter.
The body moves better.
The spirit begins to lift.

Breathing becomes easier
as eyes are open to a new brightness,
and for once, the numbness is gone.

The movie feels different
as it plays around you instead of from afar.
You are finally taking the role you deserve.

It's not lonely.
It's not empty.
There is nothing wrong with you.

Tended to, the flicker will grow,
but will also never fade.
Hope is always here.

—Hope Flickers

You yearn for the warmth.
Seek it not outside of you
but from within you.

— To Be Loved

Grief is a dear friend
for refuge when shadows reign,
and joy's glint must heal.

And when hope restores,
grief affirms its care complete
so you stand anew.

Hold duality.
Dwell in darkness, leap in light.
Both press you forward.

—The Cycle

Within lies shadow.
Souls have both darkness
and a light aglow.

Drawn from years ago
that failed to repress;
within lies shadow.

So too the days flow,
with hope for progress
and a light aglow.

Fear not the below
that calls to depress.
Within lies shadow.

With both shall one grow;
a force to harness,
and a light aglow.

A choice they bestow,
balance to caress.
Within lies shadow
and a light aglow.

—The Duality Inside

You have my safety in mind
but you are also my heart's killer—
carving out my chest and leaving me hollow.

We want the same happiness for me. For us.
But your storming ingress voids the world
with darkness cast over me. I'm swallowed.

It hurts. I can't endure the empty "what if's"
aching where you tore my bleeding heart.
My heavy body discarded to rot and wallow.

My friend, if we want our desires fulfilled
and the future to outshine our past,
we must brave and chance the light of Apollo.

I love you for your protection, Fear,
and I forgive the poor executions.
But for both of us, your path isn't one to follow.

—My Friend Fear

It's not cliche when I say, "it's me."
I changed—The past is all you dream.
You're my shadow, fear, and blight.
My child deserves new light.
For my final cease:
I forgive you.
I love you.
Thank you.
Peace.

—So Long Self

I'm standing at the precipice
of light and dark
with the monumental ask:
Do I rise or do I fall?

My heart begs for air,
for time to salve its aches.
But time also carries on.
Do I rise or do I fall?

The darkness coaxes,
"Settle with current comforts
than soar to the sun and burn."
Do I rise or do I fall?

Yet the sun warms me with hope,
helps the day shine brighter
and my love embrace tighter.
Do I rise or do I fall?

Simple are the lounging days
with purring thoughts—Life is weary
when seeking more than the now.
Do I rise or do I fall?

But so my soul yearns for truth,
to discover my inner power.
It is there. I feel it.
Do I rise or do I fall?

The journey's path is a test,
but if we fail to step forward
then there is no journey to take.
Do I rise or do I fall?

I have my answer.

You too, stand at the precipice
of light and dark
with the monumental ask:
Do you rise or do you fall?

— The Ask

She sleeps and dreams come to her;
so when she wakes with a stir
there's a fire in her belly
to tackle all that's scary.
But when she tells around
about her plans abound,
she's met with hesitation
and cries of devastation.

They say,
"Don't try—it's too hard.
You'll just fall apart.
I'm looking out for you.
Hey, it's just what I do.
How could you think you can make it?
Life isn't up for the taking.
Please don't do this to yourself.
Let those dreams sit on the shelf."

But she sings,
"I may not know where I'm going,
but I'll walk anyway.
I may not know what I'm doing,
but I'll try it with grace.
I may not know where I'm going,
I'll just find my own way.
I always do.

And so will you."

—I Always Do

Rise up to the rhythm. Who raps the drum anew?
Hammering your heart's cage; I see who it hails to.
Your deepened desires call. Do you know what dreams brew?
Your fire is not fragile. Know the beat and fight true.
Vow your vision to keep. Your valor they shall rue.
Wage on your warfare, friend, and win your treasure due.
Let not your courage cease, the drum will carry through.
Let not your sound silence, the drum beats sole for you.

—Heart's Drum

part iii

She drifts through the home of the trees; her steps a slow, delicate pace, as if she floats above the foliage that dusts the earth in color. She is older, wiser, experienced.

And yet still, she feels the same pain in her heart from all those years ago.

Her power of a chameleon has failed her, and for what reason she cannot parse.

Her colors expanded from black and blue to purple and green. Green was a color that always had her nod and do as asked when tasks arrived on her desk.

This was the way, was it not? To survive? To morph with new colors in order to adapt to the needs of others?

It was not.

Her days of green had produced remarks of high regard from peers. But her loyalty was not enough to keep her safe from a monster so infatuated with wealth. It found her at her desk and tossed her out like carnage to be cleaned up without care.

Her loyalty would never be enough for it, no matter how she craved to fit in the same world it lived by.

break control

Seek your merit not
through gilt titles on pages.
Glitter lies within.

—Recognition

So you win again, old friend;
shaming me with your lies.
Twisting my loyalty and love
to shape my own demise.

It's the hardest act to realize:
the one I play as the fool.
But with clarity comes role-shedding
and choosing to end this duel.

Though let it be known to you
I won't walk away silent,
nor forgive with, "oh, it's okay,"
for I have a larger intent.

Because karma is my friend
I gossip to when drunk with pain,
demanding proper retribution
the moment I drop your name.

"We sin and God forgives,
so party on," as you say,
but that cycle of redo
is no longer the game I play.

And while I hold the desire
to lower our spiteful debt,
know full well that to forgive
does not mean to forget.

I cannot take your plea for peace
to replay this song—"avoid drama."
Just learn from your doings, for once,
before you meet my friend, karma.

So allow me to make my entrance
and declare this dragging party over.
Because I won't be shamed again
and I like me better sober.

—Forgiveness

You come, see chances.
You fall—learn—and rise taller.
Then you will conquer.

—Caesar-like

The savage daughter
with screaming heart breaks the glass.
"The cycle must pass."

—*Generational Trauma*

Why are you like this?
I'm angry at you for this,
but also myself.

I want to tell you,
but if I do, I hurt you.
I don't want you hurt.

So what do I do?
Do I open up to you
or hide the anger?

But it has to go.
I can't contain this in me
or I will just break.

I would make it worse,
for this to bottle until
the beast is unleashed.

And what then, my love?
Will you understand my thoughts?
Will you still love me?

I am too afraid
of hurting you and being
invalid; a brat.

I care more for you
than speaking to what hurt me.
I am stuck with this.

Please understand me.
Please understand my feelings
and we can improve.

But I accept it,
if you can't see what I mean
when I speak my truth.

I feel better though,
to release the true feelings.
They are out there now.

For you to see me
you must know how I feel, Love,
or we don't work out.

Ah, I get it now.
For one to understand me
I must let it out.

If you don't like it,
if you don't understand me,
then you don't know me.

I need to be real.
Only then can I free me
from this rusty cage.

—Break

"You cannot keep me."
The torch lands on the aged home
and burns all to ash.

—Rebirth

Mindful is the soul
to not judge a book by the cover,
but to open the pages
and read the story between lines.

Yet freedom is acceptance of letting go
when the words fail resonation,
when the themes spoken disagree.
Not all books are written the same.

Not all experiences are the same.

You may love books, desire them in your home
to befriend them, understand their stories.
But you may not like all books.
And that is human.

It's a wonderful lesson,
one to take from the library, the bookstore,
and explore the world with—
where people are like books too.

—The World's a Bookstore

The world is critical enough
with all the "should's" and "should not's."
But depreciating others
through self-loathing is a nasty plot.

"My way, or the highway, dear.
What you do isn't real art."
Well, what's that mean anyway?
Different lights inspire different hearts.

"What you do doesn't work for me.
Therefore it's wrong. I know better."
Friend (do I even call you that now?),
it's not nice—sending nasty letters.

They say to err is to human,
but you're perfect, I guess,
when no one can see behind
the closed door hiding your mess.

"Free verse is too easy."
"Haikus are cop-outs."
"Third person gets 3 stars."
"No spice is a boring route."

You say it's to help me grow
to prepare me for drought,
but you battling my drum's beat
is your lame attempt for clout.

So spatter your words and dislikes.
I see who you really are.
It does naught. I like my success.
You can't taint my shining stars.

You don't have to like my poems,
my stories, my rhyme.
But cut your words with abuse
and you bet I'll write about you in time.

—Fueled by the Unsolicited

"You just can't do it."
The words smack as a rough tide,
but I smirk. "Watch me."

—Not My Doubt

Doubt rolls as a fog
against light 'til one recalls
they carry the torch.

—Only Fog

They cannot change us.
Today, always, I am me.
Always stand as you.

—Our Uniquity

part iv

Then arrived her days of purple—the color adopted when rest was no option and "hustle" was the only way to thrive. These days had fared no better than green. She fell under outside influence once more, instructing her in their own meanings of material worth and success, without considering the impact made on her health; physically and internally.

Still, she was told to continue on, and on, and on.

Until she ran. Until she escaped to the trees.

embrace rest

I loathe you, Turtle.
That race was never yours to win.
Why would anyone wait for their desires?
Why not race like the hare
to reach the magic across the finish line?
That magic brings wishes to life.

"Don't rush the progress," you say.
"Life is about the journey," you say.
Do we really have that time?

But I see you and your joy.
Time and distance are meaningless.
You know, in time, the future comes.
You know, in stride, your goal will be met.
Every step you take is a joy because
it's a step closer to magic.

No. I'm wrong.
Every step you take is a joy
because the magic is already there.

What point is there seeking magic at the end
when you can sense it around and within—
shift your mind to present joy?
Deadlines and progress are arbitrary
compared to the joy of the journey.
It's never about the destination.

Turtle, I understand now.
Because I'm tired.
I tried too much, like the hare.

I'm burned out, beaten, bruised,
watching my progress rot.
And in my forced respite I see you.
You, Turtle, catching up.
Because slow and steady
truly does win this race.

That's it. Life isn't a race.
Life isn't a rush to the end.
Because "the end" is life ceased.

Life is a garden—
building your foundation,
preparing soil, planting seeds,
and tending to new ventures
for growth and fulfilling fruit.
We must treat life every day with turtle steps.

—Turtle Steps

'Tis not sole your steps.
Progress is also made by
slowing down to rest.

—The Coin of Progress

"This world's light to see
shines from my two eyes and glee,"
my soul's grace decrees.

—*Gratitude*

It's the light of the sun
that beams on your face
with gentle warmth;
and you beam back
with your own light
that others can bask in,
and be warmed themselves.

It's the filling of one's heart,
like a steaming drink
against the frigid cold
to keep your body cherished;
an intimate embrace
from one whose soul
connects with yours.

It's the unfiltered sounds
that escape your lips and core,
echoing across the room
as your belly clenches
with a glee unraveling
your entire being into
cracked toothy smiles.

These moments are
a mystery to mankind,
when they are yet simple
to conceive in life.
Mountains need not climbed
to reach the sun and sky,
only stillness and present mind

These moments are
the little wonders,
the bliss of the journey,
up the mountain.
Not the mountain itself.
Can you see them?
Can you feel them?

They surround your path,
seeking the discovery
not only from your eyes,
but with your mind.
They make the mountain
a glorious feat to climb:
The moments on the way.

—The Moments on the Way

Child of earth, she calls.
Listen. Feel. Heart beats with trees.
Stillness: tender growth.

—Mother's Serene Embrace

Few things still matter
after time dulls the burdens
we add weight to now.

—Featherlight

Feel it grow.
Flow it through.
Let it go.

In the know,
sensing blue.
Feel it grow.

Face the woe.
Change your view.
Let it go.

Dig below.
Seek what's true.
Feel it grow.

Join the flow.
Find the clue.
Let it go.

Then you slow,
see anew.
Feel it grow.
Let it go.

—Breathe Emotion

Life is but fluid.
You don't war with the water.
You flow with the tide.

—Control

Today I am here.
Tomorrow is for later.
I control the now.

—Present

part v

And here she falls, crunching the colorful growth beneath her knees as her head shoots back to face the sky. To face the trees with warm streaks down her face and wail.

I've tried everything!

But the trees remain still. These guardians she had watched from afar for so long, that she now escaped to when all else was lost. That she risked her horrid fear of loneliness to venture out and finally meet. And only silence greets her.

Do you really have nothing to say to me? After all this time!

Silence.

I am alone! And I don't want to be alone!

The gentleness of a breeze whisks between the green. The trees shift at the touch with a quiet rustle. But still, silence.

She cowers. Her arms hold her as she trembles against the earth, forehead kissing the dirt.

Please, I don't want to be alone. I don't want to be left behind.

Her final plea meets more silence. And she surrenders. The release weighs on her like a heavy blanket.

She awaits the blanket to smother her. Suffocate her.

Instead, it comforts. Instead, she listens to the silence.

What if you don't like who you see
when I show you the real me?
What if removing this mask
is more than I can ask
to have you see the truth?

They say revealing your true soul
will draw those, like a sign on a flagpole,
to create your almighty community
filled with joyous opportunity.
But where is the proof?

The thought to start over
with new friends and a makeover
invites loneliness and fear—
that no one will show if I switch gears.
What if the real me is unpleasant?

I see souls all around me shed old skin
and rise as the titans that hid within.
The world swarms them with love
as if blessed from above.
Can I be just as effervescent?

I yearn for the same rising support,
to receive overwhelming rapport
that helps and loves—but to ask is taboo.
"Be selfless, but prioritize yourself, too."
What if the real me drives them away?

But if I do nothing and wallow as I am
then I simply run the same program
led by my old mask that I'm not valuable.
It's time for a change, something radical.
so here's a beacon lit at my life's bay.

I hope you like who you see
when I show you the real me.
Removing the mask
was the best to ask
for myself. My truth.

Oh, a ship. Coming from the sea.
And in sunlight I bask.
There's my proof.

—Open for Love

Ertha
Croons—
Love
Is
Passing
Shadows
Embraced.

—Solar Dance

"I don't think I can."
I respond, "Believe in me
who believes in you."

— When in Doubt

Friend, look what I see in your eyes:
A soul much stronger than it deems,
with strength to blind a sunray's gleams,
yet places faith in false demise.

Rise up tall and reach past the skies.
Your dream is nearer than it seems.
Friend, look what I see in your eyes:
A soul much stronger than it deems.

Weaken the fear shaking your cries,
turn those words to defiant screams.
Break this old attire at the seams,
unearthing your truth is the prize.
Friend, look what I see in your eyes.

—Your Soul's Beholder

You see missteps, falls.
I see bright change in the path.
Each step is a gain.

—Journey

How I yearn to be the voice
that liberates self from the past
for the joy of a future.

How I yearn for daylight
to warm my cheeks
and touch my lips,

To catch the whisper
of the divine voice
that welcomes my win,

And the twinkling eyes
of a soul with a fire
as lit as mine.

The journey of self
feels like a lonely trail—
but wait, why so?

Why, when I see
the sea of lingering faces
that watch my every breath?

The throngs of thoughts
that question my words
or admire my actions?

Why must the mind
desire the suffering
of a false loneliness,

When the imagination
behind our eyes
creates our own reality?

Cruel it is to settle
when it holds the power
to conquer all in its path.

And now I see
I am not alone
in my journey.

My journey connects
with others in a web
of stringing lights.

And we have our trails
blinded by the brain fog
that beds with isolation.

Now I see the path
the mind obscured from fear
of shining too bright.

How I yearn to be the voice
that liberates not just self
but all light from the fog.

—Stringing Lights

Wait. We are the same.
We live, we love, and we dream.
Why do I hate you?

—Through the Fog

And so we wind between our words
like delicate dancing steps.
Beauty is in the eye that sees,
but all I see is your shattered glass;
and you refuse to pick up the pieces
of your past, present, and future,
as you disregard my own patchwork
that I see as an art in progress.
Your shards cut when we are close,
and I'm afraid of my own glass breaking
by your thoughts in sound waves
and that disapproving stare of ice—
no, jealousy?

Oh, my dearest friend.
I share not my window with art
for you to peer in with spite.
Nor is my celebration of life
to draw a black hole between us
so you can see a "me versus you."
I share my window of the world
to show how you too, yes you,
can pick up your pieces of glass
and make art of your own.
When I next glance with my eyes,
I wish to see your true colors
that kaleidoscope with life.

Yes, I dream of a world
made up of mosaic windows,
and we are the artists
that stand together behind it;
hand in hand.

—Make Art, Not Shards

Darling, do you love me the way I am?
Broken into a million pieces.
I can't hide them. I'm sorry.
But I will try still.
For you, I will try to be perfect.
For you, I will try to be enough.

Darling, is it okay I've fallen backwards?
Stumbled so many steps back
I can't see the light ahead. I'm sorry.
But I will get up.
For you, I will stay standing.
For you, I will keep going.

But darling, what are you doing?
Here with me on my path
when you could be leagues elsewhere. I'm sorry.
But you're staying.
For me, you're helping pick up my pieces.
For me, you're helping show the light.

Darling, I feel myself changing
all because of your love.
I can see more clearly now. Thank you.
And here I stand with you.
For me, I see my worth in your eyes.
For me, I feel myself mended anew.

Darling, I understand now.
Here on this path of mine
I am not broken or lost. Thank you.
I walk with you and your love.
For us, we walk together, always.
For us, we walk as one, always.

And Darling, I will stay with you
for when your path becomes rocky too,
as you have done for me. I love you.
We see strength in ourselves and each other.
For us, we are moving forward, together.
For us, we are standing tall, together.

Together and always.

—Darling

I will carry the hammer
and make the first swing.
But I wonder, my friend,
will you swing it thereafter?

You praise my actions.
You support my methods.
But when the time calls to join,
will you swing it thereafter?

The first step is the largest
that quakes the earth beneath.
Will you step for the hammer?
Will you swing it thereafter?

And should we meet a force
that denounces our ways,
will you still take my hand?
Will you swing the hammer?

I caused the upstart, the roars,
but I need you by my side.
We are stronger together.
Will you swing the hammer?

'Cause if you really want change,
I can't do it for you.
I will make the first swing,
but will you swing it too?

Will you swing the hammer
and keep swinging thereafter?

—Hammer of Change

part vi

For the first time, the noise of the world she knows is gone. A world that, when she returns to it, will never drown her in noise again.

Because the clarity from silence, from the trees, is the loudest thing she has ever heard.

Making them happy does not mean I am loved.

Another breeze sweeps through, causing her to raise herself from the earth. Her face and hair catch in the elegant dance of the wind.

The last thing I've tried is doing what makes me *happy.*

The last thing I've tried is finding my own *color.*

Her chest swells. Her heart ignites. Lips quiver with more streaks down her face.

The last thing I've tried is finding love through loving myself.

Still she trembles, but she stands. Slowly. She raises her face to the sky once more, and stares at the strip of golden light gleaming through the trees.

The trees. Her powerful, silent guardians.

embrace self

Fresh is the rainfall air that lifts with prophecy of rebirth.
A light casts the world in vivid colors and glasses half-full as
I stretch for freedom's warm rays. Sprouting wings feels
Tangible—like a child's giggle free of public's eye, relishing a
Honey decadent on the tongue. Sweet hope. Sweet faith.

—Faith

"Time to step back, dear,"
Moon coos to her weary Sun.
"You deserve the break."

—Moonlit Respite

And when the sun comes
to break night to dawn, I'll say,
"Yes you, you did it."

—Sun on the Horizon

outro

I am now yellow.

Yellow like the sun—who warms all with her light, and shines without fear of being snuffed. Yellow, like the pure bliss of a child at play. Yellow, like the freedom of loving and being loved without shame.

My color is yellow. My true color is yellow.

And my days will always and forever be yellow.

I had always enjoyed writing poetry here and there, but never took to posting it seriously until 2020. Just as COVID was changing lives.

If you told "2020 me" my poetry would affect the lives of others—and mine—while becoming a published collection. I would've said you were crazy.

These poems are my raw thoughts and emotions to you. And I can only hope they help heal your wounds just as they helped heal mine.

These are also what inspired me to keep going and finally write the fiction series I've always dreamed of writing. Because when you prioritize yourself, heal, and grow, then the real magic of "you" happens.

Thank you for picking up this book. Thank you for giving my words the space. My love goes out to you, my family, and the writing communities who had my back since 2020 (looking at you especially, Vocal Media and Twitch fam!).

Always remember to stay true to yourself, because that's what matters most.

Your light matters. Your color matters.

You are valued and loved for who you are.

About the Author

Lindsay Sfara is an author and poet surrounded by the creative chaos that is her voice acting husband and two cats in Ohio. With her collegiate studies in international politics and foreign languages, as well as her personal journey in mental health, she is inspired by the power of self and cultural storytelling to stand up against societal influence and pursue more than the static definition of success and happiness.

You can find more of Lindsay's work at
www.lindsaysfara.com

Plus find her on social media!
Twitch: WriterLii
Instagram: lindsay.sfara
Threads: lindsay.sfara
Bluesky: lindsaysfara.com

www.ingramcontent.com/pod-product-compliance
Lightning Source LLC
LaVergne TN
LVHW010939110826
845149LV00013B/2679

* 9 7 9 8 9 9 4 1 3 6 4 0 9 *